Discovering
FAMOUS BATTLES:
ANCIENT WARFARE

Jeff Fletcher

Shire Publications Ltd.

CONTENTS

ACKNOWLEDGEMENTS

The illustrations are by Dorothy J. Davies and the cartography is by R. J. Holmes. The cover design is by Robin Ollington.

1. WEAPONS AND TACTICS OF ANCIENT WARFARE

An important point about the warfare of the Ancient period is that both technology and tactics changed relatively slowly. Thus, though the period covered by this book is nearly 500 years, there will be similarities in weapons and tactics of all the battles. For example, the scythed chariots faced by Alexander at Arbela in 331 B.C. were similar to those used against Xenophon's 10,000 in 401 B.C. and were, according to Xenophon, designed by Cyrus the Great in 550 B.C. Even as late as 54 B.C. the chariot (not scythed) was to prove a nuisance when used by the Britons against Caesar's invading Romans. On all these occasions it was, as we shall see at Arbela, tactics which defeated the chariot, and not any technological advance.

Tactical progress was faster, though still slow by modern standards. Plataea (479 B.C.) sees the defeat of the Persian army, relying on a mixture of firepower and cavalry shock, by a Greek one built round the close order infantry phalanx. Alexander the Great added cavalry shock to the Macedonian phalanx and destroyed the Persian Empire at Arbela (331 B.C.). The Macedonian phalanx itself went down to the less rigid close order drill of the Roman legion at Magnesia in 190 B.C.

Basically ancient soldiers destroyed their enemies in two ways, either at close quarters in a melee or at long range by some form of missile weapon.

The main close quarters weapons were the sword, which could range from a two-handed broadsword to the short gladius of the Roman legionary, and the spear. The spear could be anything from 6 feet long, as used by the Persians, to the reputed 24 feet of the post-Alexander Macedonian phalanx. The battle axe, often swung two-handed, was also used, and it was a lethal weapon in skilled hands as it could slice through any armour.

A short spear could also be used as a short range missile weapon — a javelin. Not all javelins could be used as spears though; for instance the Roman *pilum,* whose soft iron shaft was designed to bend on impact, was difficult to use as a fighting spear. The javelin, which relied on the unaided muscle power of the soldier, was effective only at short range. For long range firepower the ancient commander had to rely on the bow or sling.

The bows were what we today would call short bows, two to four feet long. These weapons were quite powerful, especially the composite bows made of wood, bone and sinew, which gave more penetration and longer range than a simple wood bow. The other missile weapon was the stone, or cast pellet, throwing sling. Because ammunition was easier to provide, and because the sling was better for high angle fire (for engaging targets uphill or troops behind high fortification) many ancient armies included units using both weapons.

In general, ancient units were either missile troops or close quarters fighters. However, most missile troops did carry a sword or dagger for close quarters fighting if they could not run away. Some units did have a true dual capability. For example, many Persian units, such as the Immortals, were equipped with spear and shield, and a bow as well. The Roman legion too could deliver a short range missile barrage with the pilum which could disrupt and disorganise the opposing enemy troops.

The long range hitting power of the ancient army was completed by the war engines. These weapons usually got their power from twisted sinew or hair, or in some cases a giant 12 to 14 foot span crossbow. Because of their size and complexity these weapons were usually used only in sieges where they could be built on the spot by the army's craftsmen. However, Alexander had mobile ones, though they did not appear at Arbela, and each Imperial Roman legion had its complement of them, though they were often used only to defend the marching camps.

Cavalry tactics

A major point about ancient cavalry is that they lacked one thing which the modern horseman would regard as vital — the stirrup, which was not invented until the sixth century A.D. Without the stirrup the vicious impact of a Medieval or Napoleonic style charge would have unseated most of the participants. This does not mean that cavalry was useless since the

Figure 1. Cavalry engaged in shock attack needed some kind of formation; generally a line or rectangle, Alexander's Macedonians used the more complex wedge formation seen here.

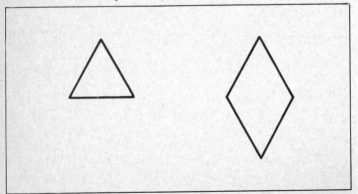

bulk of the horse was dangerous, and the man on horseback, especially when equipped with a long spear, or lance, had certain advantages. Nor did the lack of stirrups handicap those cavalry who used missile weapons such as the bow, or the javelin. It does mean, however, that the term 'cavalry charge' in an ancient battle means something less spectacular than our image of it.

Cavalry engaged in skirmishing with missile weapons did not need to stick to a particular rigid formation. Those engaged in a shock attack did need such a formation, and the most commonly used was some form of rectangle or line formation. A more complex formation, used by Alexander's Macedonians, was a wedge, in the form of either a triangle or a diamond, as in figure 1. This formation has the advantage of concentrating the shock effect on a small portion of the enemy line. On the other hand it would probably be more difficult to maintain during the charge.

Infantry tactics

The core of any ancient army was the infantryman, and one of the major weaknesses of the Persian army was its lack of good native-born heavy infantry. Their usual solution to this was to hire Greek mercenaries, such as Xenophon's 10,000. During this period being a mercenary, either a common soldier or a general like Xanthippus, was more acceptable than it is today.

The ancient heavy infantrymen, whether Greek, Carthaginian or early Roman, were very similar. They fought shoulder to shoulder, equipped with spear, sword or dagger, shield, and armour. A set of armour in this period usually consisted of a helmet, a corselet protecting the torso, and greaves to protect the legs. The standard formation was the phalanx, perhaps eight ranks deep, with the spears of the other rank protruding beyond the line of the front rank. Thus from the front the phalanx presented a hedge of spearpoints, like seventeenth-century pike units, lethal to enemy infantry and cavalry alike.

These heavy infantry could be supported by light infantry, usually missile troops, whose function it was to skirmish with, to harass, the enemy forces. They might be used to destroy enemy chariots or to drive off war elephants. They could also be used against enemy infantry or cavalry units, both to disrupt their formation and to inflict casualties. Sometimes they would be joined in this role by light cavalry units, horse archers or javelin-men. Often these light units would be auxiliaries, such as the Roman army's slingers from the Balearic Islands or the Cretan archers of Alexander the Great.

The battle array

Figure 2 shows an ancient army prepared for battle. The centre is held by the heavy infantry, whose flanks are covered by heavy cavalry prepared for shock action. Their flanks in turn might be covered by light cavalry, horse archers etc. In front of the main line are the light infantry, ready to harass and disrupt the enemy line, and prevent the enemy light troops attacking the main body.

Many variations of this pattern are possible and several of them will appear in this book. Indeed this general pattern recurs again and again long after the ancient period.

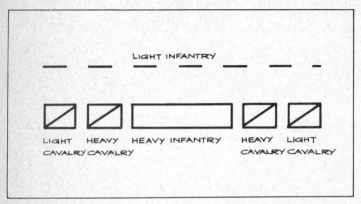

Figure 2. The traditional formation of an ancient army prepared for battle.

2. THE COMMANDERS

Mardonius

A nephew of Darius Hystapis, the king who preceded Xerxes, he commanded the expedition to Greece whose fleet was destroyed by a storm off Mount Athos. He was in disgrace after this and did not take part in the Marathon campaign. On the accession of Xerxes in 485 B.C. he regained his position as a leading general. He was one of the main supporters of the decision to invade Greece again in 480 B.C. When Xerxes decided to return to Persia after Salamis he took command of the forces remaining in Greece, and was defeated and killed the following year at Plataea.

Pausanias

The son of Cleombratus and nephew of Leonidas he was appointed Regent on the death of the latter. He was chosen to command the combined Greek army which was victorious at Plataea. Afterwards he became haughty and ambitious, seeking to become a tyrant. After his capture of Byzantium he was twice recalled for treachery (negotiating with Xerxes). He tried to start a helot rebellion in Sparta and, upon being discovered, sought sanctuary in a temple. The Spartans bricked him up in it and let him die of starvation.

Alexander the Great

Alexander was born in 356 B.C., the son of Philip of Macedon and Olympias. During his youth he was closer to his mother than his father. His first achievement was the breaking of Bucephalus, a horse whom most people, including Philip, thought unridable. At sixteen he served as Regent and at eighteen led the Macedonian cavalry at Chaeronaea. Two years later Philip was assassinated and he became king. In 334 B.C. he invaded Persia. After his victories over Darius he led his army deep into India and after his return, in 323 B.C., he caught a fever and died at the age of thirty-three.

Darius III Commodus

In 338 B.C. Ataxerxes III was assassinated and after a period of confusion his distant cousin Darius Commodus became King of Persia. His rise was assisted by the eunuch Bagoas and as soon as he established himself Darius forced Bagoas to take poison. Darius had earned a considerable reputation as a commander in border wars, but he almost immediately found himself matched against Alexander. After being defeated at Issus and Arbela he fled eastwards in the company of the satrap Bessus, but in 330 B.C., with Alexander in hot pursuit, Darius was assassinated by Bessus who proclaimed himself Great King.

Hannibal Barca

Hannibal was born in 247 B.C., the year his father Hamilcar took command of the Carthaginian forces fighting the first Punic war in Sicily. He was born into the Barcid family, one of the most powerful and anti-Roman families of the city. When Carthage was defeated Hannibal accompanied his father to Spain where he eventually succeeded to the command and started the second Punic war. After his defeat at Zama he worked to rebuild the city but in 195 B.C. he was driven out by Roman hostility. He wandered around Western Asia for thirteen years but eventually, pursued by Roman agents to Bithynia, he took poison and died in 182 B.C.

Gaius Terentius Varro

A low born citizen of the Republic, his father was reputedly a butcher. During the early stages of the second Punic war he was a member of the party opposed to the tactics of Fabius, a stand which led to his election as one of the consuls for 216 B.C. Against the opposition of his consular colleague he fought and was defeated at Cannae. One of the few survivors of the disaster, he worked hard to repair the damage and was forgiven by the Republic. Later he was ambassador to Philip of Macedon, and Syphax, King of Numidia.

Arminius

Arminius, or Hermann to give the German form, was a chieftain of the Cherusci tribe. He served with the Roman armies, accompanying Tiberius to Pannonia. His brother, who took the name Flaminius, remained loyal to Rome until his death. Arminius was forbidden to marry his chosen wife by the Roman governor Varus, but eloped with her. After his defeat of Varus Arminius continued his struggle against the Romans, blocking any attempt by them to establish themselves north of the Rhine. In the lull after one such campaign a period of strife took place within the Cherusci and during this Arminius, aged thirty-seven, was assassinated.

Publius Quintilius Varus

Varus had a typical Roman administrative career and he managed to rise gradually during the Civil War period. In 13 B.C. he was elected consul and then became a provincial governor. During his period as governor of Syria he suppressed a revolt in Judaea. When the revolt in Pannonia broke out Tiberius was sent to take charge there and Augustus appointed Varus to take his place in Germany. In A.D. 9 he was tricked by Arminius and his army was destroyed. Varus committed suicide to avoid being captured.

3. GREECE AND PERSIA

The conflict of systems

The conflict between the Greeks and Persia is the earliest war for which we have reasonable records, though these are mostly from the Greek side.

In 550 B.C. the Median empire was taken over by Cyrus, the Persian who established his rule over much of Asia. Then began seventy years of constant Persian pressure on the Greeks. The first to feel this pressure were the Greek colonies in Asia Minor, the Ionian Greeks, who were soon incorporated into the Persian empire.

This was an uncomfortable position because the Ionians, who were European, democratically governed, and had a free and disorganised religion, did not appreciate the centralised Asian government of the Persians, whom the Greeks regarded as barbarians. However, the threat of the archers and cavalry of the Persian army kept them under control, especially after Cambyses, the son of Cyrus, conquered Egypt, defended largely by Greek mercenaries.

However, in 499 B.C. the Ionians, and the Greek cities in Cyprus, revolted against Persia, ruled now by Darius. The suppression of this rebellion took the Persians six years. In general the mainland Greeks left their colonies to fight their own battle, but Athens, at this time one of the most powerful of the Greek city states, and Eretria helped briefly in 498 B.C. sending an expedition which destroyed the Persian administrative centre of Sardis. After this one brief incursion the Athenians left the Ionian Greeks, who by 494 B.C. were safely back under the Persian yoke.

The scope of Athenian help was unfortunate, too little to be of any real assistance in the Ionians' struggle, but sufficient to annoy the Great King, and make him decide to chastise those who had aided the Ionians.

The first Persian expedition came in 492 B.C. and it conquered much of Thrace and Macedon before its supporting fleet was destroyed in a storm off Mount Athos.

So in 490 B.C. (or perhaps 491 B.C. — there is some dispute about the date) a Persian fleet and army sailed for Greece. This force was not a full scale invasion, as some writers suggest, for it consisted of only 25,000 infantry and 5,000 cavalry, but a punitive expedition, though the experience would undoubtedly be useful if Darius did decide to launch a full scale invasion.

The Persians moved against Eretria, which, after a siege, was betrayed and captured. Simultaneously the Persians advanced towards Athens, their other objective, sending a force to Marathon to tempt the Athenian forces out of the city so that the pro-Persian faction could seize control and betray Athens as Eretria had been betrayed.

Athens appealed for help to the other Greek city states, but only a small contingent came, from Plataea. The Spartans, the most powerful military state, were delayed by a religious festival.

The combined Athenian/Plataean army moved out and faced the Persians at Marathon for some days. The Athenian command structure at this time was somewhat peculiar. The army was divided into ten 'tribes' each with its own leader or 'strategos' and these in turn were commanded by a 'polemarch' or war leader, but the honour of drawing up the army for battle rotated daily between the ten strategoi, one of whom, Miltiades, had an unusual battle plan and the Greeks waited until it was his day for com-

A typical Persian cavalryman, from a painting on a Greek vase. He rides without stirrups, which were not invented at this time. This type of cavalryman fought at Plataea, and similar troops faced Alexander at Arbela. Some cavalrymen might have carried a bow in addition to the spear.

mand before they attacked. Miltiades strengthened the two wings of his force, at the expense of the centre, and, moving quickly to lessen the effect of the Persian archers, broke their army after a bitter struggle. The Persian fleet and the survivors of the army returned to Persia.

Further Persian attacks were delayed by two events. The first was the outbreak of a revolt against Darius in Egypt and Babylon which took several years to suppress. The second was the death, in 486 B.C. of Darius himself. These two events created sufficient confusion to delay the next onslaught until 480 B.C. when Xerxes, Darius's successor, himself led his army into Greece.

In the Marathon campaign the Greeks had made no attempt to oppose the Persians at sea, but now Athens was a major naval power. Themistocles, who had been one of the ten strategoi at Marathon, had persuaded the Athenians to use the income from a silver mine at Laurium to build a great fleet, ostensibly for a war against the Greek island state of Aegina, but actually in case the Persians returned.

The invasion of 480 B.C.

In 481 B.C. Xerxes established his headquarters at Sardis and prepared for a full scale invasion of Greece. This was to be no mere punitive expedition like the Marathon campaign; the full resources of the entire Persian empire were to be brought to bear to crush the insolent Greeks.

Even before the invasion Persian diplomacy had won a major victory. There were many Greek colonies in Sicily, notably Syracuse, which could have helped mainland Greece with ships and men. Herodotus suggested 200 ships and 30,000 men as the possible Syracusan contribution. But these cities were faced with a challenge on their own doorstep, for Carthage was making one of her periodic attempts to dominate the island. According to the historian Diodorus this was pre-arranged with the Persians, and as Carthage was originally a colony of the Phoenicians, now the core of Xerxes's navy, this seems very probable.

In 481 B.C. the Persian army marched. The forces, both men and ships, had been gathering for four years. The size of the force is in some dispute, for though Herodotus's figure of over two million has long been discredited there are still widely varying estimates. J. F. C. Fuller suggests an original strength of 180,000 men, though a figure as low as 50,000 has been suggested. But, as even after the wastage of a year's campaigning, the losses at Thermopylae, losses in other skirmishes and the troops who returned to Persia with Xerxes, the army of Mardonius at Plataea could face the whole of Greece, the higher figure of about 180,000 seems most acceptable.

The Persian plan of campaign was fairly simple. It relied on co-ordinated operations between the army, moving down the east coast of Greece, with Athens as the first major objective, and the fleet. If the army were blocked the fleet was available to support them, or to bypass the blockage. If the fleet itself were stopped the support of the army could help it to victory.

This in its turn governed the Greeks' planning. Outnumbered both on land and at sea the Greeks needed a place where both their army and fleet could fight in a confined space, where the Persian numbers might prove a positive handicap.

The first position chosen was at the Vale of Tempe in the north, but this could be bypassed both by land and sea and the Greeks retreated southward.

The next defensible position was at Thermopylae on land and Cape Artemisum at sea, and here the Greeks faced the invaders again. The pass here was at one point only 15 metres wide, and at sea the fleet could face the Persians in confined waters.

Due to the strength of these positions neither the Persian army nor the fleet could force their way through and after several days' fighting the Persians had lost heavily both on land and at sea, though a number of the Persian naval losses were due to a storm.

Eventually a traitor revealed the weakness of the Thermopylae position to Xerxes; there was a pass through the hills, and Xerxes promptly sent the Immortals, the elite Persian infantry force, along it. Leonidas, King of Sparta and commander of the Greek army, had posted a Phocian detachment to guard this passage, but the Persians brushed them aside.

On hearing this Leonidas split his forces, sending most of the army back to clear away the Immortals, retaining only his own three hundred picked Spartans, the Thespians, and the Thebans, whose loyalty was in doubt. The force sent back failed to make contact with the Persians and retreated southward.

Later that day the news came to the fleet, Leonidas, his three hundred Spartans and the Thespians were dead, the Thebans had joined the Persians and the way south was open.

There are several monuments and epitaphs in the pass, but the most impressive is that to the Spartans, a stone lion bearing the inscription:

> 'Go tell at Sparta, thou that passeth by
> That here obedient to their laws we lie.'

The next good defensible land position was at the Isthmus of Corinth, which meant abandoning the north of Greece, including Athens and Plataea, to the Persians. While the land forces fortified the Isthmus the Persians swept south to Athens and, despite attempts to defend the Acropolis, the city was captured. The Athenians had moved their families to the island of Salamis and were unwilling to allow the fleet to retreat from there to defend the Isthmus. Tactically too the Athenians had a point; it would be easier to face the Persians in the confined waters off Salamis than in the open seas off the Isthmus. With half the fleet Athenian Themistocles had a powerful voice in the councils but eventually it was only by the Athenians threatening to sail to Italy with their entire fleet and found a new city there that they got their way. Because of this, and the tactical justice of the Athenian case, the combined fleet decided to face the Persians off Salamis.

Even so the fleet would have retreated had Themistocles not sent a message to Xerxes warning him to attack before the Greeks escaped. Next day the Persian fleet attacked, having sent one squadron round the island to trap the Greek fleet.

Half the Greek fleet was Athenian, while the major contingents in the Persian fleet were the Phoenicians, Egyptians, and Ionian Greeks. Both fleets consisted of galleys which struck their sails before battle and manoeuvred under oars only. The main tactics were to ram and sink, with the extended iron shod keel, or to lay alongside an enemy ship, sweep its deck with arrows and javelins, and board.

In the confined waters off Salamis the superior Persian numbers could not be brought to bear and after a savage fight lasting some seven or eight hours, under the eyes of Xerxes, watching from a throne on the mainland, the Persians fell back, minus some two hundred ships.

The strategic effect of the battle was considerable. The Persian plan had depended on coordinated operations, and after this defeat the fleet was a broken reed. Furthermore the Greeks now held the command of the sea, and could, if they chose, attack Persia, or destroy the bridge of boats which Xerxes had had built across the Hellespont, and thus cut him off from Persia. The Greeks could also encourage their Ionian cousins to rebel again.

Because of these considerations Xerxes decided to return to Persia, but for political and prestige reasons he could not abandon Greece entirely. He left an army under Mardonius, his senior general, to keep the Persian flag flying and, hopefully, to subdue the Greeks.

The Plataea campaign

There was no major campaigning in 480 B.C. after Salamis so the final battle to expel the invaders from Greece did not take place until 479 B.C. The size of the Persian force under Mardonius is, almost inevitably, difficult to determine. Herodotus, perhaps to magnify the Greek achievement, suggests 300,000 but a more reasonable estimate would be between 50,000 and 100,000. They were a picked force, and included some of the very best of the Persian cavalry.

13

Mardonius was master of Greece as far south as the fortified line of the Isthmus of Corinth. Most of the Greek city states north of this line had been forced into alliance with Persia. A notable exception was Athens, still defiant. However, Athens now had new rulers, for Themistocles had been defeated in the annual elections. Mardonius, realising the decisive value of the Athenian fleet to the Greek cause, offered peace to the Athenians. Until this offer was made the Spartans, the major element in the land army, had been content to sit behind the Corinth line, like Wellington at Torres Vedras, waiting for Mardonius to attack or retreat. But the threat of an Athenian-Persian alliance forced them to approach the Athenians and agree to an offensive to destroy Mardonius.

The combined Greek army seems to have reached a similar size to the Persian, but the balance of arms was different, the Greeks being mostly heavy infantry. It was divided into three contingents, Spartan, Athenian and Allied, though the Spartan and Athenian contingents actually included troops from other nearby cities.

In a sense the Greek intention to move forward suited Mardonius because he wanted a place where his superior cavalry could be brought into play. In order to hasten the Greek move Mardonius again attacked Athens, burned the city and withdrew North towards Thebes which, since the loss of the fleet, had been his advanced supply base. The Boeotian plain around Thebes was good cavalry country, unusual in mountainous Greece, which would give Mardonius a chance to use his best arm.

The Greek dramatist Aeschylus, author of a play about Salamis and Plataea (*The Persians* — this is the only Greek play to have survived that dealt with current events), described the Persian wars as a conflict between the spear and the bow and he is partly right. The Greek army of this period consisted almost entirely of 'Hoplites', heavily armoured infantry, equipped with a shield, spear and sword, and fighting in a close order phalanx. Greece was not good cavalry country and only a few states had any sort of cavalry arm. Prominent among these were Thebes and Macedon, but as both were allied to Persia their cavalry was lost to the Allied army. The Greeks were also weak in light troops, though each Spartan was accompanied by a number of Helots, or slaves, who may have served in this role. The Athenians had also developed a corps of naval archers and for this campaign they had been pressed into service on land. The Greeks were, however, still basically a close order, close quarters infantry force.

The Persians on the other hand excelled in just those arms which the Greeks lacked. The Persian cavalry, much of it armed with the bow as well as close quarters weapons, was far more manoeuvrable than the Greeks, both in campaign and on the battlefield itself.

PLATAEA

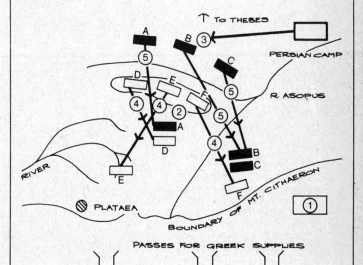

A GREEKS IN PERSIAN SERVICE
B ASIATICS
C PERSIANS

↑ TO THEBES

PERSIAN CAMP

R. ASOPUS

RIVER

PLATAEA

BOUNDARY OF MT. CITHAERON

PASSES FOR GREEK SUPPLIES

D ATHENIANS
E "ALLIES"
F SPARTANS

1 ORIGINAL GREEK POSITION
2 GREEK MOVE TO OUTFLANK PERSIANS
3 PERSIAN COUNTER MOVE
4 GREEK NIGHT MOVE
5 PERSIAN PURSUIT

15

The Persian infantry was well-equipped for firefights, for units like the Immortals, the elite infantry unit 10,000 strong, carried the bow as well as the spear. The weakness of the infantry was that it could not face a Greek phalanx in close combat. The Persians had a shorter spear, little armour and wicker shields, which gave far less protection than the metal shield of the Greeks.

These differences in the structure and equipment of the two armies governed their preferred tactics.

The Greeks, unable to cover their flanks with cavalry and under threat of disorganisation and heavy casualties from Persian missile fire, sought to close with the weaker Persian infantry and break them, as at Marathon. With its flanks properly protected a phalanx could also stand off a charge from the Persian cavalry.

The Persian tactics were basically to use their infantry to pin the enemy and cause casualties with missile fire while the cavalry prepared to deliver the decisive blow. Thus in the battle to come two very different tactical systems would clash.

The two armies made contact near the city of Plataea where Mardonius prepared to block any Greek move on Thebes. The Greek army was commanded by the Spartan Pausanias, acting as Regent for the young Pleistarchus, who had become one of Sparta's two kings on the death of Leonidas. The Greeks initially assembled on the foothills of Mount Cithaeron. On seeing this Mardonius sent forward his cavalry, under Masistius, to attack the Greeks. The Persian cavalry were, according to Herodotus, able to inflict heavy casualties on the Greeks, though they do not appear to have come to close quarters at first. After a time an Athenian bowman hit Masistius's horse and he was unseated. A force sallied out and killed him, and a fierce struggle soon developed for the body. Eventually the Persians were driven off and the Greeks were left in possession of the body.

This loss was a severe blow for the Persians, and a major morale boost for the Greeks. Because of this, and the fact that their current position lacked drinking water, the Greeks advanced on to the plain. Their plan was to attack Mardonius, now installed in a fortified camp, and drive him away from Thebes. Though the manoeuvre was completed Pausanias did not attack at once, why is not clear, and Mardonius was able to turn and face him. In the ten days that followed there were a number of skirmishes in which the cavalry and light troops of the Persians were usually victorious, and at least one large Greek supply column was totally destroyed. But the most serious blow came when Mardonius, having forced the whole Greek army to depend on one spring for water, by pushing the Athenian and Allied contingents back from the river Asopus, then raided the spring. By the time the Greeks had driven the raiders off the spring was useless. The Greeks now had no real choice but to pull back to their original position on Mount Cithaeron, but of course Mardonius knew, and would be prepared for just such a move.

The decision was taken to withdraw part of the army about a mile to an island of land between two rivers, which would provide both plentiful supplies of water, and a measure of protection against the Persian cavalry. The rest would go right back to Mount Cithaeron and cover the passes through which the Greek army was being supplied, and which the Persians had frequently attacked.

Although it would have been a retreat this move would have given the Greeks a much better position for a defensive battle.

There were unfortunately going to be a number of problems in carrying out this manoeuvre.

Firstly, because of the nature of the ground which had to be crossed to reach these new positions, the Greeks felt they had to move at night, or the Persian cavalry would be presented with a perfect target. Of all military operations a night march is perhaps the one most likely to go totally wrong. Distances and directions become confused, rocks appear to be enemy troops, and a wandering animal can cause chaos.

Secondly, military etiquette dictated that the Athenian and Allied contingents must cross in the dark! Before the move the line was formed with the Athenians on the left, the Allies holding the centre, and the Spartans on the right. However, had the move been completed as planned the Spartans would have been separated from the rest of the army, and the Athenians were then entitled to hold the right of the line. So they had to change positions with the Allies. It was therefore decided that the Athenians would wait until the Allies and the Spartans were out of the way before they moved.

Despite these problems it is barely possible that the manoeuvre would have gone off as planned, had it not been for the third complication. This was a Spartan regimental commander called Amompharetus. The Persians had earlier taunted the Spartans as cowards because they had tried to arrange for the Athenians to face the Persian contingent of Mardonius's army. There was a sound military reason for this: the Athenians were the only people to have faced the Persians, at Marathon, and survived.

Amompharetus, described by Fuller as a 'typically stupid Spartan', decided that he, and his unit, were not going to retreat because of any army of barbarians.

Because of arguments with Amompharetus it was nearly dawn before the Spartans got moving, and the Athenians had not moved at all. Only the Allies had reached their assigned position on the 'island'.

Having started late the Spartans did not have time to reach the protection of the foothills of Mount Cithaeron before the Persian cavalry were upon them. The Spartans were soon pinned and, seeing his opportunity, Mardonius sent his centre and left wing infantry to destroy them, leaving the right wing, composed of those Greeks who had joined the Persians, to engage the Athenians. This they did, and when Pausanias, hard-pressed, sent to the Athenians for aid they were unable to come. The Allies, having arrived at their assigned position were, for the moment, out of the battle.

The Spartans were in considerable danger as the Persian cavalry stood off and bombarded them with arrows. When the Persian infantry came up they did the same, building a barricade of wicker shields for cover. Behind his Persian units Mardonius deployed the Asiatic troops of his centre. This was a mistake, because the mass of Asiatics destroyed the freedom of his Persians to retreat if the Greeks attacked. This is exactly what Pausanias did, sending his troops forward against the barricade of shields. Able to get to close quarters with their enemy the Spartans began to force them back. This was the sector on which Mardonius and his picked guard were fighting. At close quarters the Persians were no match for the Spartans and they suffered heavily, and when Mardonius himself was killed by a Spartan called Arimnestus the whole force broke.

The Athenians meanwhile were engaged with the Boeotian Greeks, and as Greek was fighting Greek it was a ferocious battle, but one from which the Athenians eventually emerged victorious and the last of the Persian infantry were put to flight in the direction of Thebes.

The operations of the Allied contingent are unclear, especially as Herodotus, the major source, is prejudiced against them. They appear to have moved forward in two columns, one of which, meeting Theban cavalry in the open plain, was routed with the loss of 600 men. The Corinthians, part of this contingent, are mentioned in a contemporary poem as 'holding the centre' and it is possible that they came into contact with the Persian cavalry which had left the Spartans once the infantry came up.

The victorious Greek army swept on, and stormed the Persian army who had fled there. The casualties in the battle are impossible to determine, but the Persian losses, coupled with the death of Mardonius, effectively destroyed the Persian army.

Ten days after the battle the Greeks laid siege to Thebes, the Persian base, and it surrendered after ten days. With Greece thus cleared the Greek army and fleet were able to destroy the Persian fleet, free many of the Ionian Greek cities and end the Persian military threat.

But the battle could so easily have gone the other way. Having forced his enemy to retire from their advanced position, especially by a night march Mardonius at dawn was in a superb position, one which he showed every sign of being prepared to use to destroy the Spartans. However he blundered by sacrificing the only real advantage his infantry had, mobility to use their long-range hitting power. Once the Spartans got in close the Persians were doomed.

But in one sense the whole war was a disaster for Greece, for there were now two first rank powers in Greece, Athens the sea power and Sparta the land power. From the end of the Persian war until 404 B.C. the history of Greece was the history of the conflict between Athens and Sparta, which ended in a Spartan victory, but a victory which weakened all the Greek states.

The focus of attention was about to shift north into Macedon where, in 359 B.C., Philip came to the throne.

4. ALEXANDER AGAINST PERSIA

The rise of Macedon

The defeat of the Persian invasion was the last great military achievement of old mainland Greece. The Peloponnesian war severely weakened the two major states (Athens and Sparta), and though a third, Thebes, rose briefly to prominence under Epaminondas, who even led a Theban army to victory over the Spartans, their supremacy did not survive his death.

The incessant internal wars, often with one or both sides receiving Persian help and encouragement, severely reduced the will and the economic resources of 'old Greece'. Another even more serious loss took place, a loss in military manpower which reduced the forces they could put into the field. During the wars the Persians, by a combination of force and diplomacy, gradually destroyed one of the main achievements of Plataea — the freedom of the Ionian Greek cities.

The real military power of the Greek world moved away from cities like Athens and Sparta, to Macedon, to island states like Rhodes and to the colonies in Italy and Sicily, though the latter were already feeling pressure from the next major set of rivals, Rome and Carthage.

In the Persian war Macedon had been an unimportant state which fell quickly to the Persians. Indeed when the Persians wanted to negotiate with Athens, between Salamis and Plataea, the King of Macedon was one of their emissaries. The Greeks tended to consider the Macedonians not as real Greeks but as mountain barbarians.

But the barbarians were about to be ruled by two brilliant kings in succession. In 359 B.C. Philip emerged as king of Macedon supplanting his young ward. Philip had earlier been a hostage in Thebes when that city, under Epaminondas, had beaten even Sparta.

Picking a general called Parmenion as his right-hand man Philip gradually subdued his neighbours by force or diplomacy. The latter term included bribery: 'There is no fortress so steep it cannot be scaled by a donkey carrying a load of gold'.

In these wars Philip drilled and improved the Macedonian army until its combination of a modified phalanx and cavalry could not be matched by anything in Greece. When the opportunity arose, due to 'sacred' wars, he marched south. The decisive battle came in 338 B.C. at Chaeronaea when the Macedonians faced a combined Athenian and Theban force. The battle was decided by a cavalry charge led by Philip's eighteen-year-old son Alexander.

The result of this victory was the establishment of the Corinthian League of all Greek states, except Sparta. Philip was elected

Hegemon, or protector, and strategos, war leader of the League. He was empowered to invade Persia though the Greeks probably intended little more than the liberation of the Ionian Greek cities.

Marathon and Plataea had been the first indications that the Greeks could beat the Persians and since then there had been an even more convincing demonstration. In 401 B.C. a large force of Greek mercenaries took service with a Persian noble called Cyrus who was trying to capture the Persian empire. The force got almost to Babylon before fighting their major battle, in which they were victorious, but Cyrus was killed. The Greeks began their journey home and though the Persians tricked and killed the commanders the Greeks fought their way back through a thousand miles of hostile country, defeating every force which tried to stop them (*see* Xenophon, *The Persian Expedition*). This was a clear indication that the military strength of Persia was no longer invincible.

Secure in his domination of Greece Philip sent a force under Parmenion to establish a bridgehead on the Asian side of the Hellespont. But before this could be exploited Philip was dead, assassinated at a religious ceremony.

Alexander was young, only twenty, and his relations with Philip had not been of the best, but his ability ensured that he succeeded Philip. Some people outside Macedon doubted his ability and before he could march on Persia some of the border tribes, and the Greeks themselves, had to be cowed. The destruction of Thebes served to convince the Greeks, and in 334 B.C. Alexander was able to move his forces into Asia.

Technically this was a Greek invasion, in retaliation for the wrongs committed during the Persian wars, and Alexander was officially the elected leader of the Corinthian League. But a look at the army list reveals that the bulk of the force was Macedonian, or mercenaries under contract to Alexander, and many of the Greeks were mercenaries themselves.

The real aims of the campaign, i.e. Alexander's aims, are not clear. There is a long debate between historians as to Alexander's intentions, and the point at which he decided to conquer the whole of the Persian empire. I am inclined to think that each success led Alexander to increase his goals until by the time of his death nothing but the conquest of the whole known world would have satisfied him.

The organisation of the empire

The enemy which Alexander took on was formidable. The Persian empire stretched from the Hellespont to India in the east, and to the south it included Egypt. This gave it immense economic and manpower resources, as the Persian order of battle at Arbela was to demonstrate. Its size also gave it the same inbuilt resistance to invasion as Russia was to demonstrate against Charles XII, Napoleon, and Hitler. The Persian control of the Phoenician cities, notably Tyre, gave them a navy, which, since the destruction of the Athenian navy during the Peloponnesian war, the Greeks could not match.

Militarily the Persians still lacked one thing; cavalry they had in plenty, archers, slingers, all manner of light troops and even war elephants, but they still had no heavy infantry who could match a Greek phalanx. And the Macedonians had proved they could defeat a regular Greek phalanx. To fill this gap the Persians tried two solutions, the hiring of Greek mercenaries and the training of a force of Cardaces, or Persian heavy infantry.

The Persian empire was subservient to one man, the 'Great King', who appointed the provincial governors, or satraps, and to whom the complex administrative structure reported. This meant that in order to capture the empire it was necessary to supplant the king, either by killing or capturing him. This need for the body of the Great King was to have a considerable effect on Alexander's strategy.

The Great King at this time was Darius III Commodus, a distant relative of the previous king. Darius had built a reasonable military reputation in border wars, and one of his first acts on reaching the throne was to make the eunuch Bagoas, who was responsible for the elevation of Darius, poison himself.

Early battles

Alexander's first strategic objective was the removal of the threat posed by the Persian fleet, which could attack his rear, or transport Persian expeditions to mainland Greece. As he could not face the Persians at sea the only solution was to destroy or capture all their bases.

But before he could do this he had to defeat the local Persian forces, reinforced by 20,000 Greek mercenaries under Memnon of Rhodes. In May or June 334 B.C. he met this force when it tried to oppose his crossing of the river Gracinus. The local satraps tried to kill or capture Alexander, realising that without his driving personality the invasion would fall apart, but they were defeated. Alexander could claim his first victory against Persians, though it was only a relatively small force, and not under the Great King.

After this victory Alexander cleared Asia Minor of Persian bases, including Sardis, Ephesus and Miletus. With his land communications thus secured he could proceed to the destruction of the Persian fleet bases, before the fleet created unacceptable problems in mainland Greece for his regent Antipater, and the small force at his disposal.

The first of these bases was Halicarnassus and Alexander soon realised that the siege was going to be a long affair. One of the normal, and least costly, methods of siege was to starve a city out, but if the city is a port then naval superiority is necessary to cut off supplies. As Alexander was besieging Halicarnassus precisely because he did not have naval superiority slower processes such as mining would have to be used. This would take time, and Alexander could not afford to have his field army tied up for too long. He left a detachment under Ptolemy to conduct the siege and moved east to meet the counter attack from the Great King, which he knew must come.

Raising a full Persian army was a slow process; although the

Left: a Persian 'Immortal', the elite of the infantry, drawn from a tiled frieze. These troops, armed with a short bow as well as spear and shield, led the move around Leonidas at Thermopylae.

Right: a Greek Hoplite, or heavy infantryman, the backbone of the Greek armies in the Persian war.

empire had vast resources they had equally vast distances to travel. The mobilisation time for the vast army which Xerxes had brought against Greece was measured in years. The longer Darius waited before moving the larger his army would be. However, there were political and military arguments against delay. The longer he waited the stronger would be Alexander's military position, as fortresses, cities and recruiting areas fell into his hands. Politically too inaction was dangerous; it could provide a reason, or an excuse, for a palace revolution. Also some of the satraps, who were almost independent rulers, might decide to go over to the successful Alexander.

By October 333 B.C. Darius decided his force, which included some 30,000 Greek mercenaries, a force nearly equal to Alexander's total infantry force, was sufficient, or that he could delay no longer.

By this time Alexander was moving south into Palestine. Darius, moving from his base at Sochoi, came through the mountains and cut Alexander's supply line at Issus where he angered Alexander by slaughtering all the Macedonian wounded he found there.

Alexander turned back as soon as he heard the news, to clear his supply line and to face Darius in the decisive battle for the Persian empire. But Issus was not to be that decisive battle.

The Persians fought well, but the charge of the Companions, Alexander's elite heavy cavalry, broke through in the sector of the line where Darius was, surrounded by the best of Persian troops. Darius, seeing Alexander heading for him and deciding this battle was lost, fled, doubtless realising that he himself was Alexander's main goal.

The rest of the Persian army fought on but was destroyed. The most serious loss was that most of the heavy infantry, including the mercenaries and the Cardaces, were among the casualties, and this would seriously weaken any future army raised by Darius.

Alexander did not pursue Darius, preferring to carry on with the reduction of the Persian naval bases. These duly fell into his hands over the next year. The most serious resistance was offered by the city of Tyre. Tyre was a unique city: the citadel was built on an island, not the mainland. It took a siege of eight months, and the building of a causeway linking the island to the mainland before Tyre fell. With the capture of these cities Alexander had freed himself of a major worry, and acquired the most powerful navy in the Mediterranean.

From Tyre he moved on down the coast, heading for Egypt. Meanwhile he had received an offer of peace from Darius, offering all the lands west of the Euphrates and also Darius's daughter, but Alexander did not accept. Instead he left Darius free to raise another army while he captured Egypt and founded

Alexandria, or rather the most famous of the many Alexandrias he was to found. He also visited the temple of Ammon at Siwa, receiving, according to his own account, a mysterious divine message which he never divulged to anyone. While in Egypt he received reinforcements from home, which he integrated into his army. He was also able to organise the administration of the territories he had captured.

In the spring of 331 B.C. he moved north again to seek out Darius and the new army Darius had raised. This time he was to get his decisive battle.

The two armies

The army which Alexander led from Egypt to face Darius was an experienced and battle-hardened force. In the three years since the start of the invasion it had marched thousands of miles, fought two considerable battles, Gracinus and Issus, and conducted many sieges.

The core of the army was the Macedonian heavy infantry, fighting in traditional phalanx formation, but with one refinement, in their main weapon. This was the sarissa, at fourteen feet a longer weapon than the normal Greek spear. This phalanx normally formed up sixteen men deep, though it could be reduced to eight to lengthen the frontage. The second major component of the infantry line were the Hypaspists, three thousand strong. Their equipment is not clear, but their role was to provide a link between the main infantry formation and the cavalry on the flank. This suggests that they must have been lighter armed than the phalanx, and consequently able to move quicker, but they do not seem to have been true light infantry in the sense of skirmishing with missile weapons. This latter role was filled by Agrianians, Cretan and Macedonian archers, and Thracian javelin-men.

The function of this infantry was to pin and hold the enemy army and to disrupt it as much as possible. The decisive blow would be inflicted by the cavalry, for the Macedonians, unlike a Greek army, had developed this arm. The elite native Macedonian cavalry, 'The Companions', led by Alexander himself, would charge from its position on the right flank when the time was ripe. The left wing was usually held by the Thessalian cavalry.

Alexander's force at Arbela has been the subject of much research, notably by E. W. Marsden of Liverpool University, and can be reconstructed fairly accurately. There were 40,000 infantry, made up as follows: 9,000 Macedonian heavy infantry in six taxis of 1,500 each, 3,000 Hypaspists, and 3,000 light infantry. The rest of the infantry were mercenaries of the Greek contingents. The cavalry numbered some 7,000, the major units being the Companions and the Thessalians, each just over 2,000 strong.

Darius had had eighteen months to collect together his army, and the presence in it of Indian and Red Sea units suggest the efforts which had been made. The ancient writers offer a collection of strength figures, usually involving some nice round number such as one million men. Modern research suggests that the cavalry of the Persian army numbered 30,000 to 40,000 — a number very close to Alexander's infantry strength. There is no adequate figure for the Persian infantry, though as, with the exception of 2,000 Greek mercenaries and 1,000 Royal Guard, they were totally useless against Macedonians it hardly matters.

Two other units in the Persian army do deserve attention. Concerned by the lack of any infantry able to face the Macedonians Darius had called on the ancient tanks. His army included a detachment of 200 scythed chariots designed, according to Xenophon, by Cyrus, the founder of the Persian empire, and rescued from the depths of the royal armoury. In case these did not prove enough Darius had also acquired a few, probably fifteen, war elephants from his Indian domains. Darius hoped that these units would break up the compact Macedonian formations and create openings for his cavalry.

Properly used the war elephants in particular could have done this, and later, when the Macedonians met them in larger numbers in India and they were deployed by a commander who understood their use, the Macedonians were badly mauled. The sheer bulk of the elephant was deadly and the smell had a considerable effect on cavalry. The crew, high above the battle and protected by the howdah, could rain missiles down on to the men below with devastating effect. The major snag with elephants, especially if they were angry or upset, was their unpredictability, and a rogue elephant was equally dangerous to both sides.

With the exception of these unusual additions Persian tactics followed the pattern of earlier days, handicapped as before by the lack of a solid infantry core.

The Arbela campaign

Darius had assembled and trained his army around Babylon where it could prepare to meet any more eastward advance into the Persian hinterland by Alexander. For Alexander, despite his considerable conquests, had not really cut into the heart of Persian territory, or of Persian strength.

Alexander meanwhile moved up from Egypt and established his advanced base at Thapsacus on the Euphrates. This gave him two possible routes to Babylon, a major objective in its own right, but, more importantly, the location of Darius. The two routes were along the valleys of the Tigris and the Euphrates. The most direct was the Euphrates, but this was both a poor supply area and the expected route. The alternative was to move across to the Tigris valley, a longer, but better supplied route. This choice of route was observed by the Persian Mazaeus who had been sent to Thapsacus with a force of 3,000 cavalry to harass Alexander as he moved down the Euphrates.

Once Darius was aware, from Mazaeus, that Alexander was moving east he set off north with his army. His intention must have been to try and contest Alexander's crossing of the Tigris, and he again sent Mazaeus forward, this time with 6,000 men, to do this while the rest of his army followed on as best it could. The army established a new base at Arbela while waiting to hear from Mazaeus which crossing point the Macedonians, assembled at Nusibles, would choose. Once this was known the Persian army moved forward again to Gaugamela to await the enemy.

The battle

Darius did not waste his time while waiting for Alexander. Doubtless some of it was spent on further organising and training of his large but, by comparison with the Macedonians, un-disciplined force. But his major activity was to level the ground on which he expected to fight. This was so that his cavalry, chariots, and elephants could manoeuvre without difficulty.

On 29th September Alexander's army moved forward towards Darius, but a few miles short of the enemy they halted on a low range of hills. There were two reasons for this halt. Firstly, it gave Alexander time, and a good position to consider the composition of the enemy army, and with the large number of cavalry, the chariots and the elephants there was plenty of food for thought. Secondly, of course Alexander could hardly fail to realise that something had been done to the ground on which Darius expected to fight.

These were obviously causes for concern, especially as some Persian deserters came forward with a story that the ground had been potholed, i.e. small holes had been dug in the ground which could trip and break the leg of a horse. This would obviously have a disastrous effect on any cavalry passing over them. There is no suggestion in any account of the battle that these potholes actually existed, and indeed they would have been dangerous to Darius's own force.

At the Macedonian conference that night it was suggested that a night attack should be made, but Alexander rejected it. One reason suggested, in Arrian, is that he wished not only to win, but to be seen to win, as decisively as possible. In addition, as the account of Plataea shows, a night manoeuvre was an extremely risky business.

Darius made a mistake that night, for while most of the Macedonians slept, his Persians were under arms and at 'battle stations' for the whole night, so that by the time morning came they were tired and unhappy.

Darius had based his battle plan on what he knew of Macedonian tactics in the past. He knew that Alexander's tactics were based on the crucial charge of the Companions and to combat this he had posted 100 scythed chariots and a special cavalry force in advance of his left flank. His main battle line was composed entirely of cavalry, with the exception of Darius's own post in the centre, where there were the 2,000 Greek mercenaries and 1,000 Persian Royal Guard. In advance of this line were the special force mentioned above, the rest of the scythed chariots, the elephants, and a cavalry force on the right flank. These forces were designed to disrupt the Macedonian army before it reached the main line. The infantry had been relegated to the second line where they might possibly encourage the cavalry, or get in the way if any of them decided to bolt.

Alexander had considered the Persian dispositions and the problems created by their unusual features. He appears to have dismissed the Persian infantry as being of little consequence. The major threat was obviously the cavalry, traditionally the best Persian arm, for the chariots and elephants could be dealt with by his light troops, posted in advance of the main battle line.

If he was to carry out his normal tactics, the decisive cavalry charge, that Persian cavalry, 40,000 strong, would have to be neutralised. The method Alexander adopted has been compared to Marlborough's at Blenheim or Napoleon's at Austerlitz. It was to embroil the cavalry in a melee with smaller cavalry forces, backed up, on the right flank, by mercenary infantry. When the Persians were sufficiently committed the charge could be made. The other possible danger was the levelled ground, which might be booby-trapped.

As the Macedonian army advanced to battle in the oblique order, with left flank refused, which Philip had learned in Thebes, it moved steadily to the right, gradually pulling Darius off his prepared ground. This was not to Darius's liking and to halt it he sent forward the force in advance of his left flank. They moved forward and tried to envelop Alexander's right flank. This was playing into Alexander's hands as he was able to block them with a much smaller force. The Persian left wing commander, Bessus, made the mistake which was later to be made by Clearnbault at Blenheim, he reinforced this attack until it reached a strength of 11,000. This force, over a quarter of the total Persian cavalry, was held in check by about 1,500 Macedonian cavalry. This was because the Macedonians, who included 600 mercenary cavalry,

ARBELA

PERSIANS

A DARIUS & MERCENARIES   F LEFT FLANK CAVALRY
B 50 CHARIOTS   G RIGHT FLANK CAVALRY
C 50 CHARIOTS : 15 ELEPHANTS
D 100 CHARIOTS
E MAIN CAVALRY LINE

ASSORTED INFANTRY

MACEDONIANS

H CAVALRY & MERCENARY INFANTRY
J COMPANIONS
K HYPASPISTS   M SECOND LINE INFANTRY
L PHALANX BATTALION   N LEFT FLANK CAVALRY
                            P LIGHT INFANTRY

1 CAVALRY ATTACKS BY BESSUS
2 CAVALRY ATTACKS BY MAZAEUS
3 LINE OF SPLIT AS TROOPS TO RIGHT CONTINUE TO ADVANCE
4 SMALL CENTRAL ATTACK LAUNCHED BY DARIUS
5 DECISIVE ATTACK BY ALEXANDER, COMPANIONS, HYPASPISTS
  & INFANTRY.

were backed up by the mercenary infantry and close co-operation between the two, as recommended by Xenophon, was a combination the Persians could not break, though both sides lost heavily.

A similar action was taking place on the Macedonian left flank where Parmenion commanded. Because the left flank was refused, or held back, it took longer for the two forces to come to grips. There was no mercenary infantry on this flank and Parmenion found himself hard-pressed. The Persians overlapped him and he was gradually being surrounded. Parmenion's force, the cavalry of the left flank, two taxis of the phalanx, and their second rank infantry, was now holding, though with difficulty, 14,000 Persian cavalry. However, in doing this they had virtually stopped and a gap opened between them and the rest of the army.

Meanwhile Darius had launched his scythed chariots against the right of Alexander's line, about where the Hypaspists were located. Probably the elephants were also launched at this time though they are not mentioned in any of the sources. However, Alexander had anticipated this move and as the chariots moved forward they were met by a shower of arrows and javelins from the light troops in advance of the Macedonian line. Those who survived the bombardment were allowed to pass through gaps opened in the Macedonian line. They were pursued and mopped up by a battalion of Hypaspists.

Darius had observed the gap in Alexander's line which had been opened up by the pinning of Parmenion's force and he sent a force of Indian cavalry forward. This was a small force designed to reach the Macedonian baggage camp and rescue the Persian royal family, captured after Issus. This was a superb opportunity for Darius, for had he sent a large force through he could have split Alexander's army in half and rolled up both halves from the centre outwards. At it was, the small force he did send was seen off by some troops from Parmenion's second line who had faced about to defend against Mazaeus's force who were beginning to surround them.

The decisive moment had come. On Alexander's left flank Parmenion, almost surrounded, was holding 14,000 Persian cavalry. In the centre was a potentially dangerous gap. On the right flank Bessus, with 11,000 cavalry committed, was about to feed more in, moving them far round Alexander's right flank. Each unit Bessus fed in prolonged his line to the left, and consequently weakened what might be called the left centre of Darius's army. This was just what Alexander had been manoeuvring for, weakness in the enemy line.

Placing himself at the head of the Companions' cavalry he gathered together the rest of his uncommitted forces, the

Hypaspists to the left of the Companions, and four taxis of the phalanx to the left of the Hypaspists. In advance of the Companions were a number of light troops, who had been engaged with the scythed chariots.

The whole of this force now began to move against the weakness in the line. It has sometimes been described as a wedge formation, but a better description might be a swinging door, pivoting on the left taxis of the phalanx. The Companions on the outer edge moved fastest, through the light infantry who then moved out to cover their right flank. The Macedonians smashed into the Persian line, first the Companions, then the Hypaspists and then the phalanx units. This succession of blows crumbled the weakened Persian line and Alexander began to roll it up, heading all the time for Darius. As the Macedonians closed in, Darius, as at Issus, turned and fled.

The battle was now won, for Bessus, realising he was cut off from the army as a result of the charge, disengaged and fell back. On Alexander's left Parmenion was still holding Mazaeus and as Alexander's attack moved along the Persian line it began to approach his line of retreat and Mazaeus too fell back. Some vicious fighting took place here, as some of the retreating Persian units were cut off by Alexander and had to fight their way out.

Alexander had now beaten a Persian army three times, and Darius himself twice. All that now remained to secure his victory was to capture Darius. Over the next few months Alexander consolidated his grip on the empire, before he finally set out in pursuit of Darius, but this victory was to be denied him. He eventually caught up with Darius early next year, 330 B.C., but he was dead, murdered by Bessus.

Arbela had been a close-fought battle, and Darius, who had produced a good plan with some surprising features, might have won had he exploited the gap in Alexander's centre. However, it was the more battle-experienced Macedonians who won out, because, in the final analysis, their commander was the better general who held himself and his best troops back until the decisive moment. His great gift was a superb sense of timing and an army organised to take advantage of it.

5. ROME AND CARTHAGE

The rival empires

After Arbela Alexander took control of the Persian empire and extended it deep into India. However, when at thirty-three Alexander died, without leaving a mature heir, his empire, assembled by his own genius and personally loyal to him, broke up in disorder. Each of the leading generals seized as much of the empire as he could, and a network of warring 'successor' states, each dominated by a Macedonian aristocracy, ruled the empire.

The genius of one man could build an empire, but it could not be sustained after his death. For a lasting empire a different type of political structure was needed. This structure was to be found in Italy at Rome. Rome was a republic with, to twentieth-century eyes at least, a rather strange political organisation. The two features of this which concern us most are the consuls and dictator.

The consuls, two in number, were elected annually and were the supreme military commanders, in addition to their political duties. When they were with the same army they commanded it on alternate days. The Roman army was at this time as amateur as its commanders. There was no standing army, each consul recruited two legions of Roman citizens at the start of his campaign and trained them as he went along. There would of course be a number of men in the legion who had served before and whose individual training was good, but the teamwork needed for the Roman tactics of the day could only be learned over a long period.

The dictator was an emergency appointment for a specified period of time, during which he effectively controlled the whole republic. Both he and the consuls were subject to criticism by the senate, a body of the wisest men in the state who acted as a form of parliament.

Rome became a republic in 510 B.C. and over the next 300 years made the slow climb to dominance in Italy. This rise was not without setbacks, such as the capture and burning of the city by the Gauls in 390 B.C.

At the time when Alexander was taking the Persian empire Rome was fighting the Samnite wars, finally to gain control over most of Italy. Next came the wars against Pyrrhus of Epirus, the republic's first major foreign opponent. Pyrrhus eventually moved to Sicily and then back home to Epirus.

The stage was now clear for the series of wars which were to dominate Roman and Mediterranean history for the next 120 years. This was the conflict between Rome and Carthage.

Carthage, on the North African coast, was originally a colony of Tyre, one of the greatest of the Phoenician cities. The Phoenicians were the greatest sea traders of the ancient world. Permanent

Phoenician settlements existed on the Atlantic coasts of Spain and Africa, and regular voyages were made to Britain for Cornish tin. It is even suggested that some Phoenician traders reached as far north as Norway.

Carthage had gradually become one of the most important of the Phoenician cities, because of its central position and the domination of the others by Persia. When Alexander destroyed Tyre, Carthage became the unquestioned leader of the Phoenician world. Her main domains were in North Africa, Sardinia and Sicily, though she had never been able to establish full control over the latter island.

The first Carthaginian or Punic war began in 264 B.C. precipitated by a body of mercenaries who, seizing the city of Messina in Sicily, appealed simultaneously to Rome and Carthage for help in holding it.

The Romans were at first at a considerable disadvantage. Over the years of war in Italy they had forged an efficient land force, but they had never needed or possessed any sort of naval arm. But the major theatre in this war was to be Sicily and the Romans could not interfere with Carthaginian reinforcements to the island, while their own supply lines were permanently at risk. The Romans therefore decided to build a fleet and challenge the leading Mediterranean naval power in its own element. The Romans had no seagoing history, and tradition has it that they built their fleet on the model of a Carthaginian trireme washed up after a storm and trained their rowers on wooden mock-ups on dry land.

Facing the experienced Carthaginians the Romans lost heavily. They could not fight a conventional sea battle and win. Their solution to the problem was uniquely logical: if you are a first class land power but hopeless at sea fighting then you must turn the sea battle into an approximation of a land battle in whatever way possible. The Romans decided to rely on boarding, rather than manoeuvring and ramming, and to ensure that they could board they devised the corvus, a boarding drawbridge fitted with a metal spike. When the corvus was dropped the spike stuck into the deck of the enemy ship, locked the two together and allowed the Roman boarders to storm across.

Using these tactics the Romans, despite severe weather losses, gradually gained control of the disputed sea areas. But they suffered a severe setback when they sent an army, under Regulus, across to Africa, for the Carthaginians had the aid of a force of Greek mercenaries under the Spartan Xanthippus. In the ensuing battle Xanthippus led the Carthaginians to victory and Regulus was among the prisoners.

The war dragged on until in 242 B.C. the Romans won a major sea battle off Sicily. This destroyed the last fleet the Carthaginians could raise, and one by one their strongholds in Sicily, deprived of naval support, fell into Roman hands. One of the last to fall was Eryx, where Hamilcar Barca commanded. Next year the exhausted Carthaginians made peace, ceding Sicily and Sardinia to the Romans.

The leading family of Carthage was the Barcids, to which Hamilcar belonged, and with their influence he secured the command in Spain after the war. The Carthaginians under Hamilcar and, after his assassination, Hasdrubal gradually built a new empire in southern Spain. This expansion brought a new source of conflict with Rome who had her own ambitions in north-east Spain.

A treaty fixed the boundary between the two spheres at the river Ebro, but with one important exception. This was the city of Saguntum, south of the Ebro, but under Roman protection.

Hannibal's war

Saguntum was to be the flashpoint of the second Punic war. By 219 B.C. the Carthaginian armies in Spain led, since the death of Hasdrubal, by Hannibal, son of Hamilcar Barca, were ready. They laid siege to Saguntum, ignored Roman protests, and after eight months the city fell.

The Romans sent an embassy to Carthage but the government, stiffened by the Barcid family and the arrival of much of the loot from Saguntum, refused the Roman request that they surrender Hannibal for trial and the second Punic war began.

The Romans in one sense were in a much better position than they had been at the start of the first war, for they now had a fleet and considerable naval experience. The Carthaginians had one major new resource, their Spanish empire. But the important factor, the one which was to dominate the whole sixteen years of the war, was Hannibal, the youthful conqueror of Saguntum.

Hannibal was able to overcome one of the major weaknesses of the Carthaginian military system. The Carthaginians had little native heavy infantry and in the past had relied on mercenaries.

Throughout history there have been mercenaries and it is really only since the rise of the 'nation state' that it has ceased to be a respectable occupation. One common and natural desire of mercenaries was to be paid. If their side was winning and there was plenty of loot and regular pay the mercenaries were usually loyal, but if things got rough and pay irregular then they might go on strike or even change sides. Indeed, after the end of the first Punic war Carthage, her exchequer drained by the long conflict, could not pay her mercenaries and they mutinied.

The Carthaginians needed a new supply of heavy infantry to stand up against the Roman legionaries and the Barcids found it in the new territories of Spain. In a sense they were still mercenaries, when considered in opposition to the Roman legionary who was fighting for his own state, but there was a considerable element of personal loyalty to their commander. All the Barcids seem to have been excellent leaders of men and again and again during the next sixteen years Hannibal was to demonstrate his ability to handle men, both in the mass and as individuals. During this period Hannibal would maintain control of a semi-mercenary army composed of many different nationalities, and for most of this time the army was on Roman territory.

The second Punic war was to be of a very different pattern to the first because Hannibal seized the initiative at once. His attack on Saguntum dictated when it would start and the movements of his army dictated where it would be fought. There were to be few naval battles because defeat in one, while inconvenient, would not be fatal to Rome. The vulnerable point was Rome itself, and her Italian possessions. In the south of Italy were many Greek colonies but lately brought under Roman control, and in the north were Gauls, hostile and barely subdued. Hannibal calculated that if he could establish his army in Italy and demonstrate that the Romans could be beaten then these groups would flock to his standard. The Gauls did so, but Hannibal's attempts to detach Rome's more civilised allies met with little success, except after Cannae, though there were some who did adopt a cautious neutrality.

Hannibal assembled his army at the Spanish empire's capital, Novo Carthago (New Carthage), in the spring of 218 B.C. It included African infantry, Numidian cavalry, Balearic Island slingers and troops from many of the Celtic and Iberian tribes of the Spanish domains. It also included a corps of elephants thirty-seven strong. The full force numbered 90,000 infantry and 12,000 cavalry.

The Romans expected to fight in Spain and sent an army under Publius Scipio there. But by the time they arrived in Spain the main field army under Hannibal had gone although forces had been left under Hasdrubal and Hanno, both brothers of Hannibal, to hold the Carthaginian base.

The story of Hannibal's long march up through Spain, across the Pyrenees through southern Gaul and across the Alps is too long to tell here (for a full account see *Enemy of Rome* by Leonard Cottrell). At the Rhone Hannibal's army, weakened by detachments, desertions and casualties had been reduced to 60,000 but the crossing of the Alps cost him more than half of this force. Only 23,000 men followed him down on to the plains of the Po, though new recruits would come from the Gauls.

Before he could advance on Rome Hannibal would have to face the army of Publius Scipio, for this army, three days behind Hannibal at the Rhone, had raced back to Italy by sea and were ahead of him. The second major Roman army, under Sempronius, was in Sicily but was recalled and force-marched the full-length of Italy.

The first clash between Hannibal and Scipio, at the river Ticinus, came before Sempronius arrived. The Romans lost—their heavy infantry could not cope with Hannibal's cavalry and light infantry in open country. Scipio was seriously wounded, and only saved, according to tradition, by his son, Publius Cornelius the younger.

The first major battle came in December when the united armies of Scipio and Sempronius faced Hannibal at the Trebia. It was Sempronius's day in command and Hannibal laid his plans accordingly. He hid a picked force in a dried up watercourse, and raided the Roman camp, before breakfast, with a small cavalry force. The Romans, despite Scipio's warnings, stormed out in pursuit. The hungry Roman army formed up in conventional fashion but their major weakness began to tell on them. The Romans were an infantry force and Hannibal's cavalry soon began to force back both wings. When the picked force smashed into the rear of the Roman army it totally disintegrated and Hannibal had won his first major battle in Italy.

After the battle Hannibal moved south, but was forced to halt by weather conditions and lost all but one of his surviving elephants.

The next year Hannibal advanced again, and reached the Etruscan plain. Knowing that one of the consuls, Flaminius, was an impatient man, who could easily be angered, Hannibal laid waste much of this plain, producing a constant stream of refugees in Rome, appealing for help and protection.

Eventually Flaminius got angry enough to march against Hannibal without waiting for his consular colleague with the other army.

He camped one night on the bank of Lake Trasimene, near where the road ran along a narrow 'coastal' strip flanked by hills. The next morning he sent his army forward, believing he would catch Hannibal on the move, but as he moved through the morning mist in pursuit of the Carthaginian rearguard he was himself ambushed in marching formation as Hannibal's army swept down from the hills. The Romans lost ten men to each Carthaginian casualty in the brief engagement and Hannibal had his second victory.

In the aftermath of this disaster the Romans appointed a dictator, Quintus Fabius Maximus, whose policy was to deny Hannibal any chance of his third victory. Fabius realised that Hannibal's main weakness, given his long lines of communication, was manpower. He could recruit Gauls, who made reasonable light and medium infantry, but was cut off from his sources of heavy infantry, Spain, and cavalry, Numidia. One arm, the elephants, had already been wiped out. Fabius therefore adopted a nibbling strategy, refusing to face Hannibal in open battle but following him closely, attacking small detachments and encouraging the allied states by his presence.

This strategy gradually wore Hannibal's forces down, but at a considerable cost. Hannibal devastated much of the best country in central Italy, though when he was told that a particular estate belonged to Fabius he left it intact amidst the devastation. Most of the Romans did not understand or appreciate Fabius's tactics and there was considerable opposition including that of his second in command, Minucius.

Because of this opposition, when the dictators six months' term expired it was not renewed and the republic returned to consular government electing, in the winter of 217 B.C., L. Aemilius Paullus and C. Terentius Varro.

Paullus and Varro

The election of these two men prepared the way for Hannibal's third and most decisive victory.

They were of different backgrounds and allegiances. Paullus was a patrician or aristocrat, an associate of Fabius, from whom he had a briefing before he left to join the army. His colleague Varro was a plebeian, reputedly the son of a butcher. But more important than his social background was the fact that he opposed Fabius and Paullus on tactical grounds. These two ill-matched men were to command the major Roman army against the most dangerous enemy the republic had yet faced, and command it on alternate days.

The Roman army

The major unit of the army they were to command was the legion. The legion was a force of about 6,000 men, carefully organised and, with one major exception, well balanced. This exception was cavalry, for the legion had a minute cavalry detachment, only three hundred men. This was a permanent feature of the legion's organisation throughout its history. The real cavalry strength of any Roman army had to be supplied by allied and auxiliary units.

The infantry of the legion were divided into four units. The Velites, the light infantry, were the first to face the enemy and then came three ranks of heavy infantry. The Romans had originally operated in a traditional phalanx formation, but found it too inflexible to fight the barbarian Gauls. Gradually the 'manipular' legion evolved with the 120- or, for the Triarii, 60-man maniple as its basic sub unit. The first line of the heavy infantry were the Hastati, armoured with helmet, breastplate, greaves and shield and equipped with two pila, javelins, and a sword. Then came the Principes, armoured like the Hastati, but equipped with a thrusting spear instead of javelins, though some writers suggest they may have carried javelins as well. The Triarii, the veteran reserves armed and armoured like the Principes, provided the rear line.

In battle the maniples could be drawn up in a checkerboard pattern, to allow the Velites and auxiliary light troops to move back and forth. Also a charge could be launched by the second or third ranks while the Hastati held the enemy at bay. Or if the battle went on for a long time the exhausted Hastati could be withdrawn and fresh troops could take over. The basic attack tactic was a volley of javelins followed up by a charge and close quarters work with sword and spear.

Properly handled the legion was an extremely flexible infantry force capable of sustained pressure which would gradually wear the enemy down. It was not the sort of force which won sudden spectacular victories, like Alexander's Companions had done, but given time and space in which to work it would destroy any infantry force it met. Unfortunately lacking cavalry and under amateur and inexperienced commanders it often came to grief against Hannibal's surprise tactics.

Carthaginian tactics

The tactics of the Carthaginians were much less stylised. There were two reasons for this: firstly, in 'grand tactics' the genius of Hannibal often managed to produce something new, and secondly, on the level of minor tactics the diversity of nationalities in the Carthaginian forces meant that each contingent had its own ideas. One reason for Hannibal's success was his ability to use each contingent in the role for which it was best fitted. Thus his Gauls, undisciplined but very brave for a short period, were used for the first shock while the less spectacular but steadier Spanish and African infantry were held in reserve. By the time of Cannae some of these latter looked like Romans because Hannibal had made use of the spoils of the Trebia and Trasimene to equip them.

But the most important units of his army, especially when compared to the poor quality of their Roman opponents, were his cavalry, mostly Numidians from North Africa. The Romans had no local answer to them at all, and when they did eventually defeat Hannibal at Zama one of the vital strokes was delivered by a force of Numidians allied to Rome.

By the time of Cannae Hannibal was without elephants, but they were not missed.

The campaign of 216 B.C.

By the summer of 216 B.C. Rome, despite her already massive losses, had managed to raise eight Roman and eight Allied legions, a force of about 90,000 men. Hannibal's army with the prestige of victory, had swollen to 50,000 but most of the new recruits were Gauls, who were not as valuable as veteran infantry or cavalry. Hannibal had 10,000 of the latter arm, and 40,000 infantry.

There had been a certain amount of outpost bickering during the winter, but the first real move of the campaign was made by Hannibal who seized the Roman depot of Cannae, while the consuls were still arguing and licking their fresh levies into legionary shape. The capture of Cannae was a boon to Hannibal especially if, as Livy suggests, he was so short of supplies that his Spanish troops were on the verge of deserting.

Conversely it placed the Roman force which had been observing Hannibal in a very difficult supply position. This led to the consuls' army moving forward earlier than might have been wise in order to recapture Cannae.

Almost as soon as the two armies came into contact, for Hannibal's main force had stayed around Gereonium, an incident occurred which strengthened the determination of Varro to seek an early battle. A clash between foraging parties and patrols escalated and the Romans had much the better of the confused fighting which followed. Paullus, whose day in command it was, stopped the conflict escalating into a full scale battle into which the Roman army would be fed piecemeal, especially dangerous as the fight was on good cavalry country. Over the next few days Hannibal made several attempts to tempt the Romans into a disorganised attack by pretending to abandon his camp. These were a failure, due to the influence of Paullus, which further widened the breach between him and Varro.

Hannibal, short of supplies, decided to move to the Apulian plains around Cannae. The Romans followed him and the opposing armies camped a few miles apart on the banks of the river Aufidius. The territory here was good cavalry country, a fact which produced more conflict between Paullus and Varro, especially when Roman foraging parties were attacked a few days after their arrival. Retaliation against these pinpricks was prevented by Paullus, who was commander that day, which only made Varro even more determined to fight Hannibal as soon as possible to prove just how wrong his aristocratic Fabian colleague was.

The battle

Hannibal, whose intelligence information seems to have been very good, had a clear idea of the men he was facing and laid his plans accordingly. He had few worries about the probable course of events on the wings, feeling sure that his cavalry, equal in numbers to the Roman and Allied cavalry opposing them, would soon disperse them. His major worry was the infantry where his 40,000 men were outnumbered two to one, and in addition many of his infantry were Gauls. At the Trebia the Gauls had formed the centre of his line and had gradually been forced back, which had allowed his better flank units to wheel inwards and hit the Romans from both sides as they followed up disorganisedly. He decided to manoeuvre for a similar outcome and formed his Gauls and Spaniards up in a bulge or wedge facing towards the Romans, while his elite Africans formed the flanks of the trap.

This was a double envelopment manoeuvre, which could produce tremendous results if it worked properly. It was also dangerous, for two reasons. Firstly, if something went wrong with the Gauls they might disintegrate before the wings folded inwards, leaving him without a centre. Secondly, he was allowing the Romans a central position from which they could switch troops round in interior lines (see figure 3) more quickly than the Carthaginians. Indeed that same year both these things happened to a Carthaginian army under Hasdrubal facing Scipio in Spain.

The two armies formed up for battle with the Roman right and Carthaginian left resting on the bank of the river Aufidius. The Roman right was formed by the Roman cavalry, then the infantry, whose left flank was protected by the Allied cavalry. Facing them, on Hannibal's right, were the Numidian cavalry, then the infantry, covered on the left by the Spanish and Gallic horse. In advance of both armies were the light troops, skirmishing as usual.

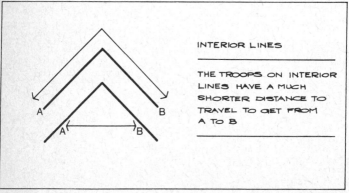

INTERIOR LINES

THE TROOPS ON INTERIOR LINES HAVE A MUCH SHORTER DISTANCE TO TRAVEL TO GET FROM A TO B

Figure 3. If Hannibal's wedge collapsed, then the Romans would have a position on interior lines, which they might exploit to destroy him.

40

CANNAE

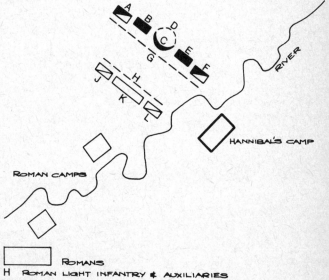

 CARTHAGINIANS
A NUMIDIAN CAVALRY
B AFRICAN INFANTRY
C GALLIC & SPANISH INFANTRY – ORIGINAL POSITION
D GALLIC & SPANISH INFANTRY – FINAL POSITION
E AFRICAN INFANTRY
F GALLIC & SPANISH CAVALRY
G LIGHT TROOPS

ROMANS
H ROMAN LIGHT INFANTRY & AUXILIARIES
J NATIVE ROMAN CAVALRY
K LEGIONARY INFANTRY
L ALLIED CAVALRY

Varro is said to have packed the legions close together, by narrowing or abandoning the gaps between the maniples, thus destroying their manoeuvrability.

The first contacts were made by the cavalry wings, with the bloodiest fighting coming on the river bank where the Romans, led by Paullus, faced the Gauls and Spaniards. Lacking room to manoeuvre it quickly degenerated into a shambles in which men leapt, or were dragged, from their horses and fought on foot amid the milling animals. This sort of fight was hardly Roman style and after a short time they fell back, leaving the Carthaginians to reform and exploit their victory.

The fighting on the other wing was much more open, where the Numidians, specialists in fast saddleless riding and javelin work, were opposed to the Allies. According to Livy, who is however biased against the Carthaginians, the confusion here was increased by a force of Numidians who pretended to desert to the Romans, and then, using swords hidden under their cloaks, attacked them from behind. The result here was the same as on the other flank, though it took longer and the threat of an attack by the Gallic cavalry before the Allies finally broke.

Hannibal now had both his cavalry wings ready and eager to seal the rear of his trap. But these flanking skirmishes, bitter and, to Hannibal, valuable as they were, could not decide the battle — that could only be done by the infantry in the centre. Here at first the Romans had the better of the struggle. The Gauls and Spaniards could not stand up to the steady pressure of the legionaries and after a short time the wedge was beaten flat.

The pressure continued and the centre was forced back. At the start of the battle the two infantry lines were almost certainly of similar length but the Roman line gradually contracted until the whole force was facing the Carthaginian centre. As the centre fell back the Romans were sucked into the vacant space, where the fighting was easier. Also the flanks of the infantry line, seeing their cavalry defeated, would tend to edge inwards. Thus did the Romans fall into Hannibal's trap. As they moved deeper into the Carthaginian centre the Romans gradually lost formation and packed closer and closer together. As their individual tactics depended on having plenty of swinging room this was very dangerous.

When the Romans were well committed, disorganised, and beginning to tire, Hannibal closed his trap. The relatively fresh African troops, equipped with Roman armour and weapons, wheeled inwards and began to drive into the flanks of the Roman infantry, packing them even closer together. A skilful general might just have been able to extricate the Romans at this point but there was still one blow to come. Hannibal still had his cavalry and when they crashed into the rear of the Roman infantry they quickly degenerated into a struggling mob. There was no escape, with the Gauls and Spaniards holding them in front, the veteran Africans driving in from each flank and the cavalry to the rear.

Cannae was the costliest Roman defeat of the war, for very few of the infantry escaped. 50,000 to 70,000 of them died that day, along with about 2,500 of the cavalry. Among the Roman casualties were many prominent people, notably Paullus the consul who, refusing a chance to escape, died with his troops. Along with him died eighty men of senatorial rank. Varro, with a small group of horsemen, escaped to Rome. The Carthaginians often crucified generals who failed, but the senate congratulated Varro for 'not having despaired of the Republic'.

Hannibal's casualties were much lighter, about 6,000, two-thirds of whom were from the centre wedge. He had planned his victory carefully, using his knowledge of the enemy commander and the fighting capabilities of his mixed army. He had found a way to let the slow steady advance of the Romans take place without them doing too much damage. He had taken a calculated risk and been rewarded with a classic and complete victory.

He had of course been helped by Varro who, determined to prove his superiority to Paullus, had made a total hash of the battle, first by crowding his infantry together and then by letting them drive deeper and deeper into the centre of the Carthaginian army without flank cover. That such a man could be given command of an army revealed a dangerous weakness in the Roman system.

The wasted victory

Hannibal had won his decisive victory and destroyed a major Roman army; it now remained for him to exploit that victory.

The army which had been destroyed was the major field army. There were other Roman forces but they would need to do a lot of marching before they could be combined into a force capable of facing Hannibal. Meanwhile, the way to Rome was open. A picked force of cavalry and light troops could have been sent in advance of the main army. News could travel only at the speed of a man riding and while it is unrealistic to assume that a military force could move as fast as a single man the Carthaginian vanguard could have been at the gates of the city within a few hours of the first news of the defeat.

Livy describes the scenes in Rome when the news arrived and the citizens were expecting Hannibal's Numidians at any time. It is impossible to predict what would have happened if they had come but the city had little left but determination. Effective control of the city rested in the hands of Fabius for, with one consul dead and the other struggling to reorganise the wreckage of his army, the ex-dictator was the only man with any prestige left. But as time passed and the Carthaginians did not come the Romans gradually calmed down and began to recruit a new army.

Hannibal had made what was to be the decisive mistake of the war. Instead of striking for Rome at once he lingered in the area of the battle. There were good reasons for this: firstly, an army which has just fought a major battle is never really in condition for a fast move, and secondly, there were still two Roman camps with about ten thousand survivors of the battle, most of whom were forced to surrender after a couple of days. But these troops, and the ransom Hannibal hoped to get for the Romans, having set the allies free, were trivialities compared with the prize he could have had.

Immediately after the battle, as Hannibal's commanders clustered around him, Maharbal, his brilliant cavalry commander, pleaded to be released with his cavalry for a drive on Rome and promised that if Hannibal let him go then he, Hannibal, would be dining in Rome within five days. Hannibal refused, saying that he needed time to think and to rest his troops. Maharbal told Hannibal that while he could win victories he did not know how to exploit one. It was a fair charge; Hannibal threw away the real possibilities of his victory.

After a few days delay Hannibal did start north towards Rome, but that few days delay was enough. He was able to pick up a major prize, the city of Capua, the second largest city of Italy. Capua decided to desert the Roman alliance and their defection brought over many of the smaller cities of the Campanian plain This was the major result of Cannae, and the only major defection of Rome's allies in the whole course of the war. But in no way could the defection of Capua be compared with the capture of Rome, which would have ended the war.

6. ROME AGAINST THE BARBARIANS

From Cannae to Augustus

The war with Carthage continued for fourteen years after Cannae. It was a very peculiar sort of war. The disaster of Cannae finally convinced the Romans that they could not face Hannibal in the open field and no more major battles were fought against him. The Romans gradually gained the upper hand in Spain, led by Scipio, the son of the man who had faced Hannibal at the Trebia.

Eventually, after the capture of Novo Carthago, Hasdrubal decided to join his brother Hannibal in Italy, while he still had a reasonable army under command. In the winter of 208 B.C. Hasdrubal crossed the Alps into Italy. The Romans were greatly alarmed, for Hannibal had been a terror for the last eleven years and now a second member of the dreaded family was approaching with a second army.

But the threat was removed by a stroke of luck and a brilliant manoeuvre. A letter from Hasdrubal to Hannibal explaining his plans, fell into the hands of Claudius Nero, the consul watching Hannibal's army in southern Italy. Nero decided on a risky manoeuvre, and leaving a force to watch Hannibal he marched north with a picked force to join his consular colleague opposing Hasdrubal.

Nero managed to conceal his arrival from Hasdrubal until the latter was unable to avoid a battle with the reinforced army. After a fierce battle Hasdrubal was defeated and died fighting with his troops. As soon as they had rested Nero's troops moved south again, taking with them a grisly trophy of their victory. This was the head of Hasdrubal which, hurled into Hannibal's camp one night, served to tell him that his reinforcements would not be coming.

Eventually the Romans decided that the best way to get Hannibal out of Italy was to force the Carthaginians to recall him by threatening Carthage itself. This decision was not taken easily and Fabius was one of the leaders of the opposition to the scheme, and the appointment of the young Scipio to the command.

In 204 B.C. Scipio and his army crossed to Africa and were joined by one of the Numidian princes which gave them the rare luxury of a reasonable cavalry force. After a few small battles the Carthaginians decided, in 203 B.C., to recall Hannibal and his army to Africa.

The decisive battle took place next year outside the town of Zama and for once the Romans won the cavalry combats on the flanks. After a long struggle the Roman infantry too were victorious and Carthage was forced to sue for peace.

This was not the end of the long conflict for though Carthage was destroyed as a military power she remained a major commercial one. Eventually, prodded by the orator Cato who ended every speech he made with the phrase 'Carthage must be destroyed', the Romans found a pretext, in 149 B.C., for attacking Carthage. The city stood a siege for three years but was eventually stormed by another Scipio. The city was burned, many of the inhabitants slaughtered, the rest sold into slavery, and the city levelled.

Rome had increased its power so much that the effort to destroy Carthage was matched by the destruction of Corinth in the same year.

In about 80 B.C. a step was taken which would radically change both the military and political structure of Rome. The general Marius reorganised the army as a long service, sixteen to twenty years, professional force, looking to its generals rather than the state for its rewards.

As he was completing this reorganisation Marius clashed with Sulla, a rival general, and this began a long series of civil wars. Marius and Sulla fought for ten years. After their deaths came the rule of the 'Triumvirate', Pompey, Caesar and Crassus. After the death of Crassus Pompey and Caesar fought and Pompey, defeated, fled to Egypt where he was assassinated.

Caesar returned to Rome but in 44 B.C. he was assassinated by a conspiracy led by Brutus and Cassius. The conspirators were destroyed by Mark Antony, one of Caesar's lieutenants, and Octavius, Caesar's adopted son. After they had disposed of the conspirators these two quarrelled and in 31 B.C. they met in the sea battle of Actium. Octavius emerged victorious and in 27 B.C. he was proclaimed Emperor of Rome.

The republic which had fought Carthage to a standstill was now dead in name, though it had been dead in fact since Marius reorganised the army.

The Roman empire and Augustus

Octavius, or Augustus as he became, was the first emperor of the Roman empire. But the empire was not his personal creation, as Alexander's had been, nor would it disintegrate at his death as Alexander's did. The empire was, in large part, the creation of the republic, and a very disorganised creation at that. Some of it had been acquired as a result of the Punic wars, and Julius Caesar had added much of Gaul while preparing, and as part of his preparation, for the inevitable conflict with Pompey. Pompey himself had added the province of Cilicia, the coast of Asia Minor, as the only way to suppress piracy there. Several territories were acquired not by conquest but by gift, left to the republic by their kings. This was how the republic acquired Pergamum and Bithynia.

The establishment of an official empire with an emperor at its head meant little more than that the governors of the various provinces reported to the emperor rather than the senate. The empire included the whole of the Mediterranean coast and under Augustus imperial policy aimed at the consolidation of a Mediterranean based empire. Augustus left a testament at his death setting out what he thought should be the frontiers of the empire. His successors tended to regard these as minimum, rather than maximum, limits. Some provinces were very secure — once the initial conquest was over Greece and Egypt gave little trouble, but Palestine ruled under Roman supervision by native kings erupted in A.D. 70 and needed a heavy commitment of Roman resources to subdue it again.

But the provinces which were the most troublesome, and the biggest drain on Roman resources, were some of the frontier ones. During his conquest of Gaul Caesar had fought a number of battles, often to protect Gaulish allies, against marauding Germans, and on several occasions he had conducted a 'reconnaissance in force', north of the Rhine. Under the dying republic the normal frontier between Roman civilisation and German barbarism, as the Romans viewed it, was the Rhine, with the occasional expedition north if the barbarians got too restless. This was a similar system to that adopted by the British on the north-west frontier of India, known to some military historians as 'Butcher and Bolt'.

Augustus did not regard the Rhine as a satisfactory frontier and as a long term plan decided to push forward to the Elbe in Germany, and move the Balkan frontier to the Danube. This would give more depth to the empire, in terms of distance from Rome, and thus reduce the chance of any incursion actually reaching the centre of the empire. It would also make the frontier more rational, and, by removing some of the kinks, shorter.

Both these thrusts were eventually to fail, though both had considerable initial success. The Danube attack foundered with only one tribe left to defeat when in A.D. 6 a revolt broke out in the 'secure' provinces of Pannonia and Illyria in the Roman rear. This revolt took four years and fifteen legions to subdue and Augustus died a few years later.

The Germans

The thrust into Germany was halted by the Germans themselves. Descriptions have been written by both Caesar (*The Conquest of Gaul*) and Tacitus (*The Germania*) of the Germans at about this time and these are worth considering.

Although I have written of the 'Germans' this is really a convenient shorthand for a mass of tribes with a similar cultural, racial, and linguistic background. Tacitus gives a description of the various tribes, though as he was writing to contrast the pure blooded, clean living Germans with the decadent Romans of his day he may be regarded as biased.

The Germans were not a settled people, preferring a semi-nomadic life. Although they did do some farming and therefore did settle for a few years their poor farming methods and large herds of cattle meant that they soon moved on. This semi-nomadic way of life, coupled with inter-tribal conflicts and pressure from other tribes to the north and east, was what caused some tribes to move south of the Rhine, which brought them into conflict with the Romans. Another cause of conflict was that the Germans actually liked fighting, considering it a much more interesting way of passing time than agriculture or any sort of constructive pursuit. The later Roman empire would make use of this by enlisting large numbers of German troops into the army, another parallel with British colonial practice. The fact that their chiefs held their office on account of their valour also contributed to their liking for warfare.

Augustus's campaigns

During Augustus's early campaigns against the Germans his forces did on occasion reach the Elbe. His general Drusus did so in 9 B.C., but was unable to cross. The biggest expedition of all came in A.D. 4 and 5 under Tiberius who, supported and supplied by a fleet which had sailed round the coast and up the river, crossed the Elbe and began to pacify many of the tribes between the Rhine and the Elbe. Unfortunately it was at this moment that the Pannonian and Illyrian revolts took place and Tiberius and many of his best troops were sent there. The Romans in Germany fell back on the Rhine as the major defence line, though they maintained a 'presence' north of it.

Tiberius was replaced by Varus, recently governor of Syria, an unfortunate appointment. He was not really the sort of man to control a frontier province, no matter how peaceful it might seem. Varus came into conflict with Arminius, a chieftain of the Cherusci, formerly a subordinate of Tiberius in Pannonia and now attached to Varus's headquarters staff. Arminius had studied Roman military organisation closely and believed he could defeat a Roman force, in the right sort of battle.

In the summer of A.D. 9 Arminius, convinced that he had sufficient support from his fellow Germans, prepared for his battle. During the summer Varus's main force, three of his five legions, were stationed on the Weser between the Rhine and the Elbe, but their winter quarters were on the Rhine itself.

Arminius arranged for a small revolt to break out in September as Varus was preparing to move to his winter quarters and persuaded Varus to move against this uprising on his way home.

The disaster of the Teutoburger Wald

In the other three battles considered in this book the two sides have been fairly evenly matched in organisation and technology, but this is not the case in the conflict between the Romans and the Germans.

The Roman army, already one of the best organised forces in the ancient world at the time of the conflict with Carthage, had developed even further as a result of the experience gained in that and subsequent wars. The Germans by comparison were by far the worst organised and equipped force to appear in these pages.

Firstly of course they were not a united nation, but a loose confederation of tribes, each under a few chieftains. The mere raising of a reasonable army was a major achievement, and the next problem was to keep them from fighting each other for long enough to beat the Romans.

A German tribesman, drawn from a carving on a tombstone. He is typical of the men who wiped out Varus, though no two tribes would have looked alike. Cavalrymen would have been very similar.

49

Their equipment was poor, armour was almost unknown. Some chiefs would no doubt have armour, gifts from the Romans, but to wear this in battle could well have been taken as a sign of cowardice. Indeed the average German warrior wore very little, perhaps only a short cloak. The usual weapon for both cavalry and infantry was a short light spear, called a framea, which could be used both for close quarters fighting and as a javelin. Some footsoldiers carried light javelins as well as a framea and some, particularly chiefs, might have a sword or a heavier spear.

Tactical formations were rudimentary, tribal wedges delivering charges which could not be sustained for any length of time being the order of the day. One advanced tactic which they had developed was the 'brigading' of elite and fit infantry with cavalry for mutual support.

The legion by contrast was now a balanced and experienced force, the like of which Europe would not see again until after the Middle Ages. The reforms under the late republic had made it a long service permanent professional force with a solid backbone of centurions, i.e. senior NCOs, and professional officers.

The paper strength of a legion was ten cohorts, each of six centuries, each nominally of one hundred men, making a total of 6,000 infantry. In fact each century numbered eighty, producing a total of 4,800. The Roman cavalry strength was only about 120, but each legion had auxiliary cavalry permanently attached. Although they all fought in the line many of the legionaries were skilled craftsmen, such as carpenters and blacksmiths, who could provide many services, like the building of siege equipment.

The armour consisted of helmet, breast and backplate and extra protection for the shoulders and stomach. The shield was semi-cylindrical, made of wood edged in metal. The major change from the time of Cannae was in the main offensive weapon. The distinction between Hastati, Principes, and Triarii had gone and so had their different weapons. Each legionary now carried a gladius, a short broad-bladed stabbing sword of a Spanish style, and two pila, though more of these were available for a sustained firefight. The Velites, the legionary light troops, had also disappeared and skirmishing was now the province of the auxiliaries.

The legion fought methodically, a volley of pila to disrupt the enemy formation, at a range of about twelve paces, then the charge. There had been a steady improvement since the wars with Carthage and the legion was now much better drilled, more flexible and better led. Nothing illustrates the methodical Roman style better than the legion's invariable practice of building an entrenched camp at night, to protect it in hostile country.

Varus had at his command three legions which, encumbered

with camp followers, totalled some 20,000 and with this force he set off to quell the uprising arranged by Arminius, who still accompanied the Roman force.

When the army had been on the march for a few days Arminius and his men disappeared to spring their trap. The terrain along Varus's route was difficult for he had to pass through the Teutoburger Wald, a large and dense wood on irregular ground broken up by many deep gullies. There had been a period of heavy rain and in some places the ground was now swampy.

The Romans, encumbered by camp followers and all the baggage they were moving from summer to winter quarters, made slow progress in this difficult country, watched all the way by German scouts.

A heavy rainstorm, making the ground greasy and slippery, gave Arminius his opportunity and his troops began to close in and hurl javelins at the Romans. Thus began the three days struggle which is known as the battle of the Teutoburger Wald. The heavily armed and armoured Romans were at a huge disadvantage in the slippery close confines of the wood and they lost heavily until eventually they were able to fortify a camp and settle down for the night.

The next day they made better progress at first. Many of their wagons and other impedimenta were burned or abandoned, and, knowing what to expect, they were in rather better formation. When they eventually fought their way out to open country they must have been very relieved.

But there was more forest to come and once the Romans got back among the trees the Germans were able to close in once more. The Romans again lost heavily but were again able to survive until nightfall.

On the third day they moved on again, but another heavy downpour completed their disorganisation. Arminius chose his moment carefully and his lighter troops closed in once more on their clumsy opponents.

The cavalry, led by their commander, were the first to break, though this is hardly surprising as they must have been even more helpless than the infantry in the wooded terrain. When the Germans closed in on them the infantry resisted as best they could but were eventually annihilated. Varus and many of his officers committed suicide rather than surrender and the whole strength of three legions died with them.

Varus had been completely outgeneralled and his army had been tempted into totally unsuitable country. He had only himself to blame, for he had been warned that Arminius intended treachery, but had chosen to ignore the warning. Arminius had made use of his time with the Roman forces to observe their weaknesses and had planned to trap them in unsuitable country where they could not deploy, and fight properly.

Though it seemed severe at the time, and Augustus could be heard lamenting 'Varus, give me back my legions', the Romans were able to recover the situation. The Pannonian and Illyrian troubles were almost over and Tiberius was recalled to Germany with many of his best troops. The Germans did not risk a major onslaught across the Rhine. The Rhine, however, was established as the frontier and the Roman armies crossed it only on punitive and trading expeditions.

As a result of Arminius's victory the idea of controlling Germany as far as the Elbe was abandoned, and the Germans were denied the benefits of Roman civilisation.

BIBLIOGRAPHY

The best starting point for a study of ancient warfare is the classical texts. The major one dealing with the conflict between Greece and Persia, and the Plataea campaign, is *The Histories* of Herodotus, who was born in 484 B.C. and would have spoken to men who fought on both sides of the war.

For Alexander's invasion Arrian's *Anabasis Alexandrensis* is available in Penguin as *The Campaigns of Alexander.* Material is also available in the biography of Alexander in Plutarch's *Lives,* and in Diodorus and Quintus Curtius.

The Carthaginian war is covered by a section of Livy's *History of the Roman Republic,* published in Penguin as *The War with Hannibal.* Livy himself drew heavily on the *Histories* of Polybius who, having been born in 203 B.C., consulted many people who lived during the war.

Much material about the Germans comes from Caesar's *Gallic Wars* and Tacitus's *Germania,* both in Penguin, but the actual account of the Teutoburger Wald comes from the *Roman History* of Dio Cassius.

All these sources have weaknesses, usually indicated in the introductions or notes, but for a general survey of ancient historians Stephen Usher's *The Historians of Greece and Rome* (Hamish Hamilton) is recommended.

There is an abundance of modern sources — *Decisive Battles of the Western World* by J. F. C. Fuller covers Plataea, Arbela, and the Teutoburger Wald. Similar coverage can be found in *The Decisive Battles of the World* by Creasy. Leonard Cottrell's *Enemy of Rome* (Pan) covers the Punic wars within the framework of a biography of Hannibal.

There are dozens of biographies of Alexander, a recent and readable one being *Alexander the Great* by Peter Green (Weidenfeld and Nicolson). This draws heavily on E. W. Marsden's *Gaugamela* (Liverpool University Press), this being the alternative and more cumbersome name for Arbela. This is a superb and excellently researched source, and one could wish for similar works on other battles.

The bibliographies of all these works will provide further suggestions for reading, and for a more general history of the period the relevant volumes of the *Cambridge Ancient History* should be consulted.

INDEX

54

Some titles available in the 'Discovering' series

Abbeys and Priories (35p)
Antique Firearms (25p)
Archaeology in Denmark (40p)
Archaeology in England and Wales (40p)
Artillery (30p)
Banknotes (30p)
Berkshire (20p)
Bird Watching (30p)
Brasses and Brassrubbing (30p)
British Cavalry Regiments (35p)
British Military Badges and Buttons (35p)
British Military Uniforms (30p)
Castles in England and Wales (75p)
Caves (30p)
Christian Names (30p)
Christmas Customs and Folklore (30p)
Churches (35p)
Comics (30p)
Derbyshire/Peak District (30p)
Devon (20p)
Dorset (30p)
Ecology (30p)
Edged Weapons (30p)
Embroidery in 19th Century (30p)
English Civil Wargaming (30p)
English County Regiments (25p)
English Customs and Traditions (30p)
English Furniture 1500-1720 (35p)
English Literary Associations (30p)
Epitaphs (30p)
Essex (30p)
Famous Battles: Ancient Warfare (40p)
Famous Battles: Marlborough's Campaigns (30p)
Famous Battles: Peninsular War (30p)
Folklore of Birds and Beasts (30p)
Footsteps through London's Past (30p)
Forests of Central England (30p)
French and German Military Uniforms (40p)
Gardening for the Handicapped (30p)
Ghosts (30p)
Harness and Saddlery (30p)
Herbs (30p)
Hill Figures (35p)
Investing Your Money (30p)
Kings and Queens (35p)
Life-boats (30p)
Leicestershire/Rutland (30p)
Local History (30p)
London Curiosities (30p)
London for Children (30p)
London - Statues and Monuments (25p)

London's Guilds and Liveries (40p)
Lost Railways (40p)
Militaria (30p)
Military Traditions (30p)
Modelling for Wargamers (30p)
Model Soldiers (30p)
Monuments (35p)
Mottoes (40p)
Narrow Gauge Railways (30p)
Norfolk (20p)
Northamptonshire (25p)
Oil Lamps (30p)
Old Bicycles (30p)
Old Board Games (40p)
Old Buses and Trolleybuses (30p)
Old Motorcycles (30p)
Orienteering (30p)
Pantomime (35p)
Period Gardens (30p)
Playing-Cards and Tarots (30p)
Railwayana (30p)
Rules for Wargaming (40p)
Schools (35p)
Sea Shells (30p)
Ship Models (30p)
Somerset (30p)
Space (30p)
Staffordshire (30p)
Staffordshire Figures (30p)
Stained Glass (35p)
Stately Homes (30p)
Statues in C. and N. England (25p)
Statues in S. England (30p)
Suffolk (25p)
Surnames (30p)
Sussex (30p)
Theatre Ephemera (35p)
This Old House (25p)
Traction Engines (25p)
Victorian and Edwardian Furniture (30p)
Walks in Edinburgh (30p)
Walks in Hertfordshire (30p)
Walks in Oxford and Cambridge (30p)
Walks in the Chilterns (30p)
Wargames (35p)
Warwickshire (20p)
The Westward Stage (45p)
Wild Plant Names (30p)
Wiltshire (30p)
Worcestershire/Herefordshire (30p)
Yorkshire - West Riding (30p)
Your Family Tree (35p

printed by C. I. Thomas & Sons (Haverfordwest) Ltd., Press Buildings,
Merlin's Bridge, Haverfordwest, Pembrokeshire.